YOUR KNOWLEDGE HAS VALUE

Bibliographic information published by the German National Library:

The German National Library lists this publication in the National Bibliography; detailed bibliographic data are available on the Internet at http://dnb.dnb.de .

Imprint:

Copyright © 2016 GRIN Verlag, Open Publishing GmbH
Print and binding: Books on Demand GmbH, Norderstedt Germany
ISBN: 9783668340817

This book at GRIN:

http://www.grin.com/en/e-book/343236/english-as-a-foreign-language-in-japan-a-case-study-of-factors-affecting

Ian Akbar

English as a Foreign Language in Japan. A Case Study of Factors Affecting Second Language Acquisition

GRIN Publishing

GRIN - Your knowledge has value

Since its foundation in 1998, GRIN has specialized in publishing academic texts by students, college teachers and other academics as e-book and printed book. The website www.grin.com is an ideal platform for presenting term papers, final papers, scientific essays, dissertations and specialist books.

Visit us on the internet:

http://www.grin.com/

http://www.facebook.com/grincom

http://www.twitter.com/grin_com

Table of Contents

Mr. T: A Case Study of Factors Affecting L2 Acquisition in the EFL Context of Japan

It is a common practice in Japan to instruct company employees in the English language for overseas assignments, business trips and conventions or conferences. Participants generally study conversation or business English. However, not all participants have equal opportunity to partake in the above mentioned events; the organizations of which they are a part, have the final say as to who participates and who does not. This being the case, some participants may find themselves required to participate in an activity (i.e., learning English), which is in addition to their regular duties, for which they may or may not be called on to utilize. For some participants engaging in such an activity may be seen as burdensome, for others, it is an escape from the daily pressures of their respective duties. In terms of second language acquisition (L2), those participants who are able to participate in overseas business trips, coupled with formal instruction appear to make the most gains. Conversely, those who do not participate in such events, even when coupled with formal instruction, appear to fossilize or plateau, if they do not recognize some other use for L2, either personally or professionally. The purpose of this case study is to examine the factors affecting the L2 acquisition of one specific individual located in Japan, in order to determine how and if the participant's level of communicative competence can be improved upon. This case study utilizes oral classroom work, informal taped interviews and participant observation of an individual student and draws on the available linguistics literature to present possible implications for instructors working with individuals in similar EFL circumstances.

L2 Acquisition: Case Study

Context

The participant was Mr. T. He was an average, middle-class, false beginner, 37 years of age. He was a company employee in Japan, who has been working at the company for the past 9 years. Personally, Mr. T was a very easy-going, though slightly introverted individual, who has expressed a certain amount of dissatisfaction with his work. He was overworked, spending up to 12 to 14 hours a day at the office. He also had never been abroad for business and didn't know that he would go abroad in the future. Therefore, though he may be able to utilize his English skills in the future, in the short-term he doesn't see any particular use for his acquisition.

Mr. T was unmarried and although currently seeing someone, expressed misgivings concerning his relationship. Generally speaking, he was not satisfied with his relationship. He believed that his partner didn't understand him and was generally impractical, insecure and unreasonable in her outlook on life. This situation appeared to cause Mr. T a great deal of distress, confusion and even depression. The situation concerning Mr. T and his partner provided a shared point of reference, we both were involved in relationships with partners who seemed very similar. Due to the fact that we were approximately the same age, it allowed us to talk about something which was of great importance to both of us and allowed for a more relaxed repoire between us.

Mr. T previously studied English in jr. and sr. high school as well as in university. He mentioned that he was interested in English in jr. high school at first, but lost interest because he didn't get a chance to use it and he didn't like the teaching method. He also didn't like English studies in university and, therefore, didn't study. He also attended conversation classes for 18 months at his other work location. In addition, he attended another conversation class for 30 minutes a week which started in April of 2004 and finished in October of the same year. Therefore, Mr. T's length of study was approximately 12 years since the age of 12. The participant was a member of a company class which I taught in 2003/4. The setting was comfortable. The class was private. The lesson duration was approximately 50 minutes and occured once a week. To that point, Mr. T used English twice in his life, when he was abroad for approximately 7 days in total. Sometimes he used English in a Filipino hostess bar in Tokyo.

Lastly, it should be mentioned that Mr. T is Japanese and was careful not to make mistakes, display ignorance and was not particularly interrogative. These are all cultural traits and Mr. T greatly improved in these areas, I believe, because the class was private and therefore he felt he could take more risks and talk about issues that were of more importance to him personally.

Level of Communicative Competence

Assessment of Mr. T was done in the initial class using a check sheet in an informal interview scenario, by asking the student pre-formulated questions dealing with personal information (i.e., name, residence, family, etc.), general information (i.e., date, high school/university, childhood, national problems, etc.), work-related information (i.e., position, work-related problems, areas for improvement, etc.) and hypothetical information (i.e., conditional questions regarding money or living abroad, etc.). His responses and the number of times the question had to be repeated were recorded. His responses determined his language level. This individual was initially rated at L in October of 2003, which indicated (according to the levels created by my sponsoring agency) that the participant could engage in simple conversation (i.e., greetings, hobbies, etc.), however, didn't understand general grammar enough. This letter grade roughly corresponded to a TOEFL level of 300. At that time, his overall speech fluency was described as being between poor to fair; on a scale from excellent to poor. Also at that time, he stated that his long-term goal in the L2 was for engaging in conversation while on overseas business trips. He was unsure as to whether those conversations would involve business or just general conversation. No short-term goals were stated. In January and April of 2004, Mr. T again received a letter grade of L for his overall fluency. In July of 2004, he received a letter grade of J, which roughly corresponded to a TOEFL level of 400.

Macro-Skill Use

Listening

Mr. T had problems with listening, especially to dialogues which were read only by one speaker. I believe that he had problems differentiating exactly who was saying what, which impeded his comprehension. He also had difficulties listening to dialogues spoken at natural/native speed. However, he had much less difficulty listening to taped dialogues or dialogues read at less than natural/native speed. He showed a marginal improvement in his listening ability between January and July of 2004.

Speaking

Mr. T had minor problems in the area of prosody (i.e., the flow of his speech was not smooth). I believe this was due to the fact that he was unsure of himself and was afraid of making mistakes.

Reading

Mr. T's reading ability was fairly good. He did tend to slow down when he encountered unfamiliar words, but this is only natural.

Writing

As the class was a general conversation class the focus was on oral communication. Therefore, the skill of writing was not actively taught.

Strengths and Weaknesses

Body Language

Mr. T's use of body language was very good. His use of body language included facial expressions, which he used to communicate various emotive states (i.e., happiness, confusion, understanding, shock, etc.) He also utilized his hands and shoulders to add emphasis or to demonstrate the fact that he didn't know.

Pronunciation

Mr. T's pronunciation was generally very good. With, of course, the exception of words he was unfamiliar with and words which offered combinations of the consonants w, r, l, f, (i.e, world, relief, year, etc.)

Grammar

Mr. T's grammar was his greatest weakness. His greatest grammatical weakness was verb conjugation or incorrect verb use (i.e., using have instead has, start instead of starts, don't instead of didn't, like instead of liked, hear instead of listen, take instead of took, drove instead of drive, etc.). Followed by his use of prepositions (i.e. to, for, etc.) However, once he was aware of some errors he was able to self-correct. He also had minor difficulties with articles (i.e., omitting a, an and the).

Lexis

Mr. T's vocabulary improved from the beginning to the end of the class. However, he sometimes had problems recalling appropriate words or terms. (i.e., he used, broken instead of sick, useful instead satisfactory, take instead of buy, busy of the highway instead of traffic jams, sure instead of certain, blood sister instead of sister-in-law, speak instead of talk, etc). He was sometimes able to self-correct. He also used Japanese when he was unaware of the proper vocabulary in areas of which he was unfamiliar (i.e., using the Japanese word for grave; ohaka, okairi nasai instead of welcome home, toro instead of tuna, hotondo instead of almost, etc.)

Relevant SLA Theory

According to Ellis (1985, 1994), situational factors are indirect determinants of the rate of SLA and also of the level of proficiency achieved, but they do not influence the sequence of development, and affect the order of development only in minor and temporary ways. (EDLA 423, Topic 2.2 Principles 2004) This situation helped to explain the relative unimportance of the setting and situation in the case of Mr. T. It also suggests that his grammatical and lexical fossilization was only temporary. Therefore, with a change in his situation, Mr. T would show some improvement.

However, as mentioned by Ellis, factors relating to motivation and personality do determine the rate of SLA and the level of proficiency achieved. The learner's first language influences the order of development (although not in major ways), but it does not affect the sequence of development. (EDLA 423, Topic 2.2 Principles 2004) This suggests that since Mr. T was unmotivated by his situation, his acquisition was impeded. It also suggests that his personality may be a detriment to that acquisition. And, that his use of Japanese in areas in which he was unsure were not indicative of any lasting problems in acquisition.

According to Lightbown (2000), a learner cannot achieve native-like (or near native-like) command of a L2 in an hour a day. (EDLA 423, Topic 2.2 Principles 2004) Since Mr. T, only received lessons for 50 minutes a week from myself and basically had received the same amount of lesson time in all his twelve years of exposure to the L2, it was not surprising that he did not achieve communicative competence.

Brown (2001) mentions the importance of meaningful learning which is closely connected with his theory on communicative competence which stresses real-world use. He states that meaningful learning will lead toward better long-term retention than rote learning. (EDLA 423, Topic 2.2 Principles 2004) Unfortunately, Mr. T was not exposed to much meaningful learning. He had very few opportunities to use the language and had only practiced it inside a classroom with a limited amount of speakers. Also, referring to Brown's anticipation of reward and intrinsic motivation, Mr. T didn't see any potential reward in his language study as he didn't even know if he would ever receive an opportunity to utilize his skills. (EDLA 423, Topic 2.2 Principles 2004) This circumstance adversely affected his level of motivation in acquiring the L2.

Due to limitations on study time brought on by work constraints the participants strategic investment was very limited. As Brown states successful mastery of the second language will be due to a large extent to a learner's own personal 'investment' of time, effort, and attention to the second language in the form of an individualized battery of strategies for comprehending and producing language. (EDLA 423, Topic 2.2 Principles 2004) Mr. T simply didn't have enough time or motivation to develop proper learning strategies.

Brown asserts the importance of self-confidence and risk-taking. (EDLA 423, Topic 2.2 Principles 2004) Mr. Takyama did not demonstrate any serious lack of self-confidence or unwillingness to take risks, in the classroom. However, not observing him outside the classroom, I am unable to say whether or not he would demonstrate these tendencies. Perhaps, being in the classroom, alone, with a person he was comfortable with allowed him greater freedom than he was usually exposed to. I remind myself that the participant was Japanese and thus, generally speaking, tended to be an introverted learner who was risk adverse.

L2 Acquisition: Case Study

It could very well be that the structure of Mr. T's native language (i.e., O, S, V) was interfering with his acquisition of the L2 (i.e., S, V, O). What Brown refers to as the Native Language Effect. (EDLA 423, Topic 2.2 Principles 2004) The participant's overgeneralization at the grammatical and discourse levels were, no doubt, affected by his L1 and are indicative of fossilization of an interlanguage norm for this learner.

In terms of listening, in relation to the rate of delivery, according to the LING 462 course notes, language learners must learn to understand normal fast speech by being exposed to authentic language as much as feasible. (LING 462, Topic 7.2 Listening Skills 2004) The participant, due to the fact that he was in an EFL context, within a Japanese speaking company, did not have the necessary exposure to authentic language and a variety of speakers that would have enabled him to consistently improve his listening ability.

In relation to speaking, since the pedagogical environment was located within an L1 environment, and the fact that different languages have different rhythm patterns as stated in the LING 462 course notes, transferring the rhythm pattern from the first language is one of the key aspects in perception of foreign accent. Therefore, second language speakers import their intonation and rhythm patterns into the L2. (LING 462, Topic 7.2 Listening Skills 2004) Consequently, the participant's inability to improve his listening/speaking ability was compounded by the location of the pedagogical and extracurricular physical environment.

Implications

The preceding section on relevant SLA theory suggests the following implications in the case of Mr. T. With a clear awareness of exactly when and in what situation he would be required to utilize the L2, a more meaningful form-focused approached could be taken. With increased levels of motivation Mr. T's acquisition rate would dramatically improve. With more time invested in the L2, Mr. T's level of communicative competence should improve. With a change in setting (i.e., the location of his class to an L2 setting) or more frequent changes in setting (i.e., business trips to an L2 speaking country), Mr. T's grammatical and lexical fossilization would be eliminated.

Professionally, the above implications have varying likelihoods of implementation due to the EFL setting and the uncertain future nature of international business. First, it would be extremely difficult to obtain and exact time and circumstance under which the participant would be required to utilize his L2 skills, therefore making it extremely difficult, if not impossible to formulate a form-focused action plan. It would be possible to hypothesize such variables, but such an exercise could hardly be called realistic since they may not happen at all. Therefore, since an instructor would not be able to ascertain the parameters of the long-term goal, it would also be difficult to formulate a short-term teaching approach, other than one that was more general. This was the approach that was being taken at that time.

Also, since the long-term goal could not be established, it would be difficult to increase the student's motivation, which I believe to be absolutely essential for him to improve his communicative competence in any setting (i.e., EFL or L2) Lastly, since the participant was pressed for time on a daily basis, even if a long-term goal could be established, it was unlikely he would have been able to find extra time to commit to his studies.

Though, perhaps, his company would have allowed him that extra leeway if an overseas assignment was impending. But, that is pure speculation at this point.

Of particular interest to this case study was Mr. T's relationship to his partner. It remains unknown as to how much or whether or not the stressful relationship with his partner had any effect on his language acquisition ability and his mental state. This particular company class did have another participant who was single and whose relationship with his partner was less than satisfactory. This individual also displayed similar interlanguage fossilization characteristics to Mr. T. He had a similar educational background and also had never been abroad, nor did he know when or if he would. Their respective communicative competence levels were similar.

The other six participants of the class were all married and demonstrated reasonable rates of improvement, with the individuals who did participate in overseas L2 contact, or interaction with L2 speakers in the L1 context, demonstrating the greatest rates of acquisition. The married participants seemed to have very stable personal lives. Could this fact be a determining factor in L2 acquisition? Further research would seem to be in order to verify or dismiss such a claim.

Conclusion

The case study of Mr. T demonstrates how a combination of factors affects L2 acquisition in the EFL context of Japan. Of particular importance is the level of a learner's intrinsic motivation for L2 acquisition. The above analysis, although far from complete due to the present scope of this exercise, suggests that an individual student must be understood as, both part of his/her cultural group as well as individually. An examination of the available literature showed that there are reasonable explanations for the behaviours observed and that it is possible to overcome the limitations of those behaviours. Though implementing those changes may be extremely difficult. Finally, the above examination suggests that there may be an important extenuating factor (i.e., quality of personal relationship) which affects a participants' level of intrinsic motivation, which should be more carefully explored in future studies.

L2 Acquisition: Case Study

Bibliography

EDLA 423: Second Language Acquisition: Applications (Sem 2) – Online Course Notes,

Topic 2.2: Principles, 2004. University of New England, Armidale, NSW. Retrieved 24

August 2004 from http://online.une.edu.au/

LING 462: Second Language Acquisition: Theory (Sem 1) – Online Course Notes,

Topic 7.2: Listening Skills, 2004. University of New England, Armidale, NSW.

Retrieved 24 August 2004 from http://online.une.edu.au/